For Sue

The publisher thanks Jenny Magnes, PhD, for her expert review of this book.

Library of Congress Cataloging-in-Publication Data

Names: Peot, Margaret, author, illustrator. | Title: The science of light : things that shine, flash, and glow / Margaret Peot.
Description: First edition. | New York : Holiday House, [2022] | Includes bibliographical references. | Audience: Ages 3-6
Audience: Grades K-1 | Summary: "Dramatic paintings reveal the sources of light, both natural and manmade, and encourage children to look around and observe"
—Provided by publisher. | Identifiers: LCCN 2021058628 | ISBN 9780823448722 (hardcover) | Subjects: LCSH: Light—Juvenile literature.
Classification: LCC QC360 .P433 2022 | DDC 535—dc23/eng20220311
LC record available at https://lccn.loc.gov/2021058628

ISBN: 978-08234-4872-2 (hardcover)
ISBN: 978-0-8234-5607-9 (paperback)

THE SCIENCE OF LIGHT

Things That

Shine,

Flash,

and

Glow

MARGARET PEOT

HOLIDAY HOUSE ● NEW YORK

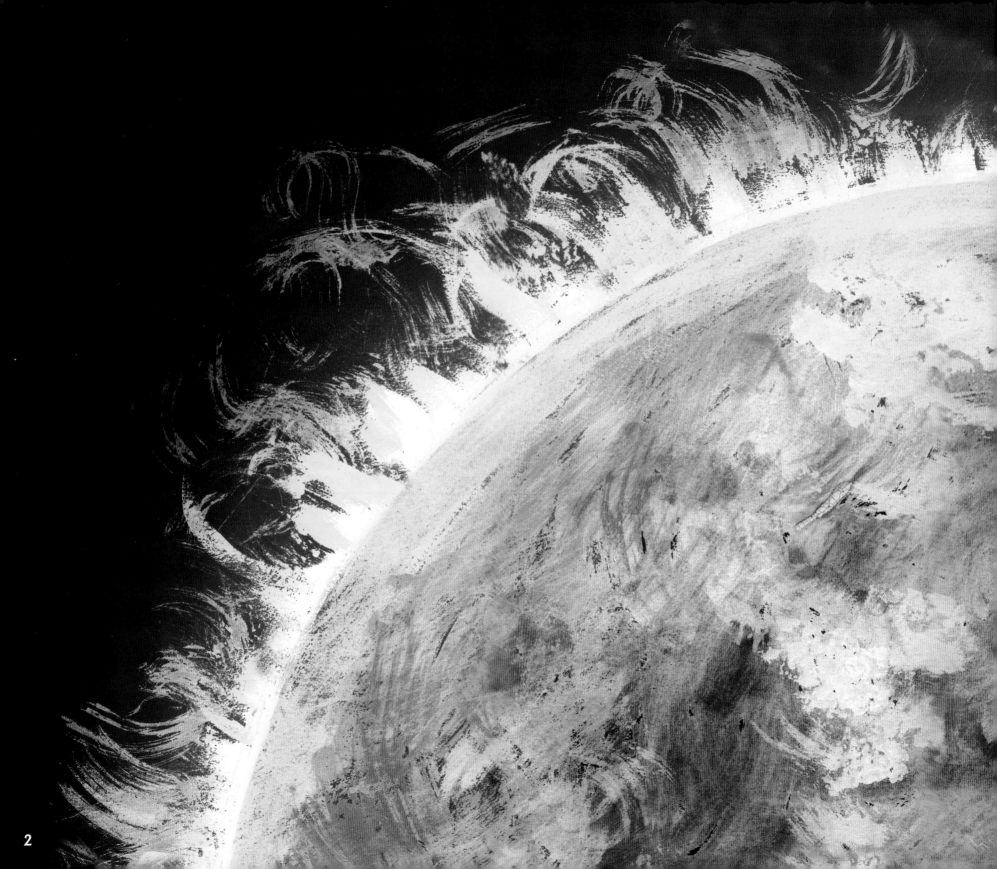

Light lets us see what is around us.
Where does it come from?

Sun shines.

Aurora borealis (uh-RAW-ruh baw-ree-A-luhs) glimmers.

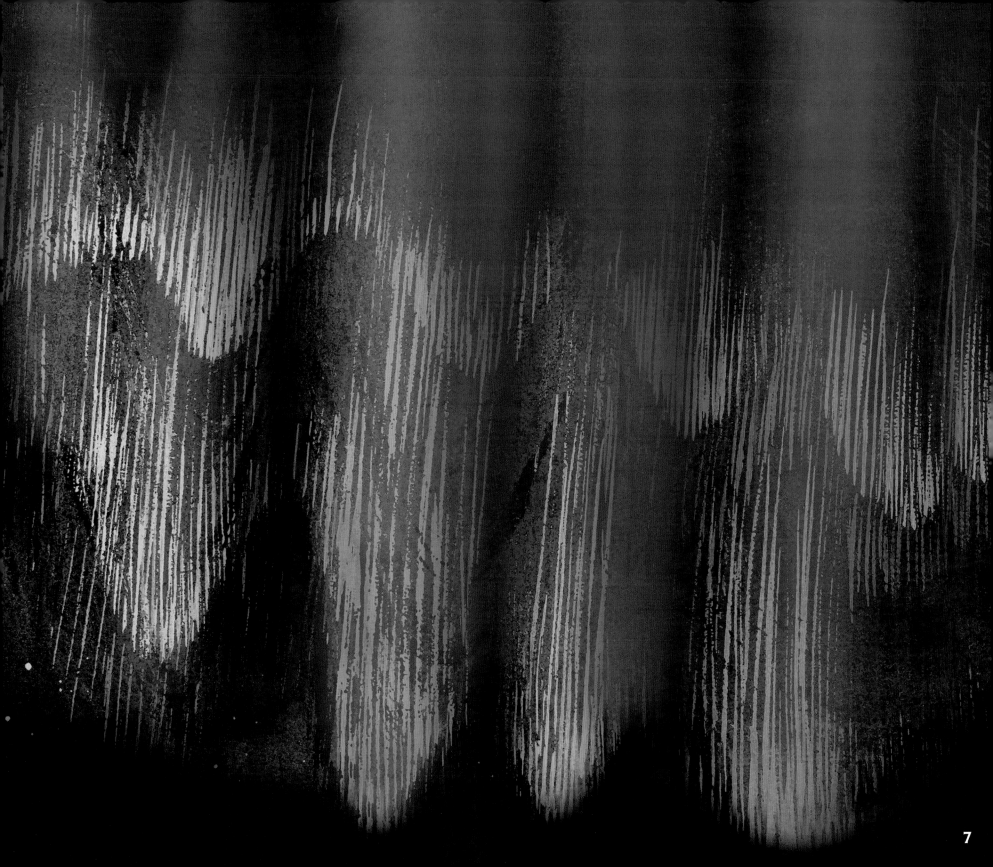

Lightning flashes.

Fire warms.

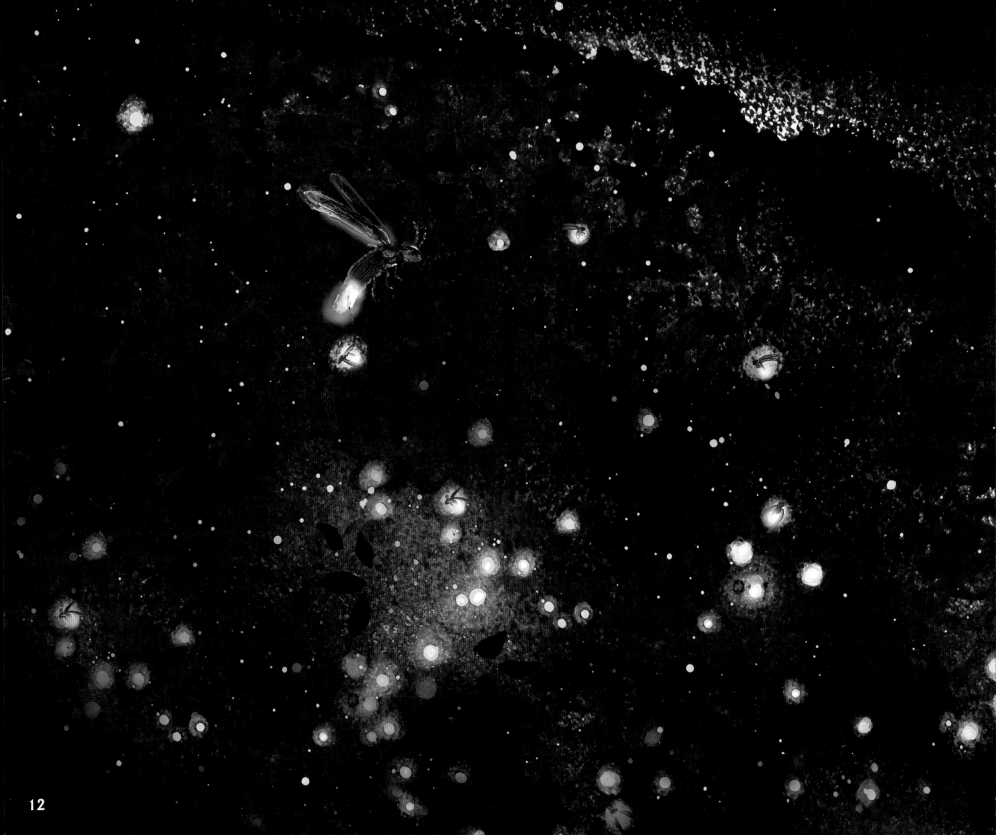

Fireflies flicker.

Mycena singeri (meye-SEE-nuh sin-JE-ree) gleam.

Clusterwink snails blink.

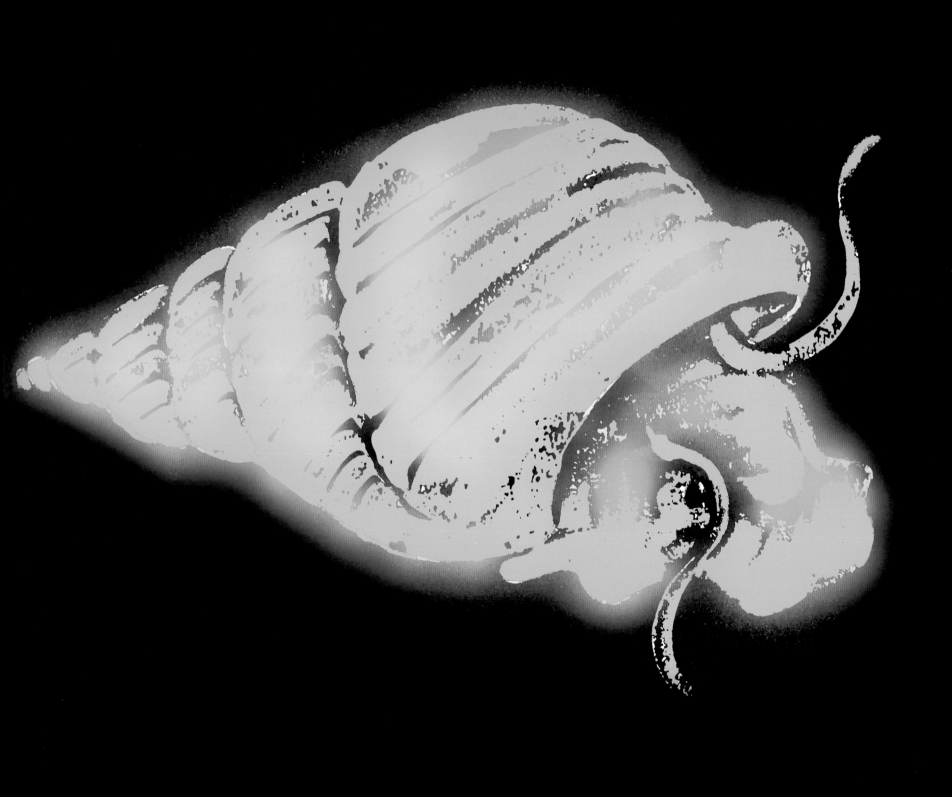

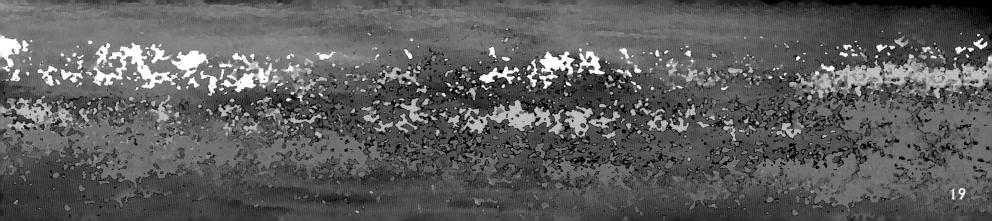

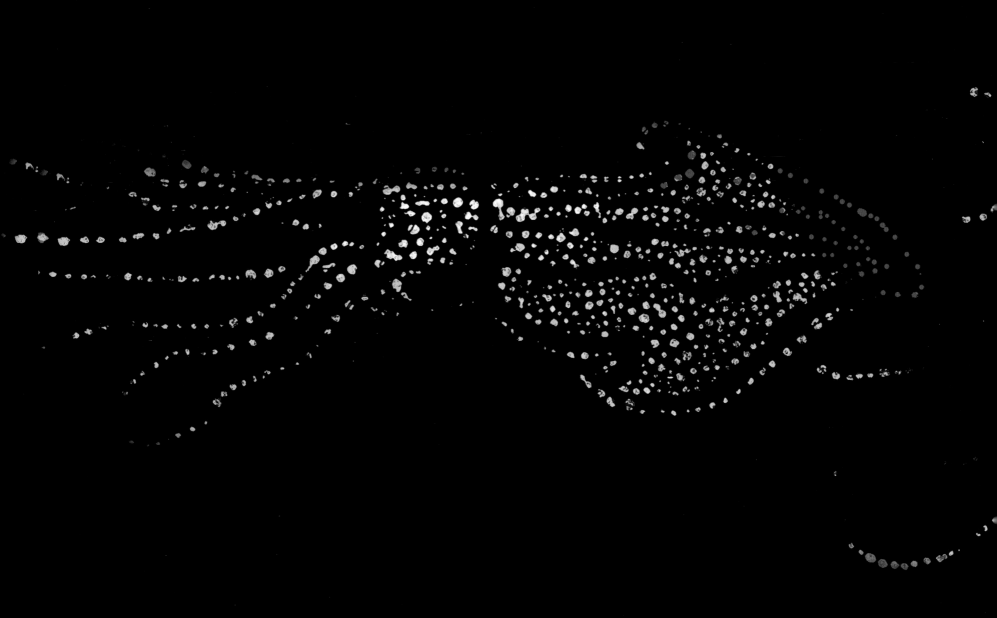

Firefly squids light up.

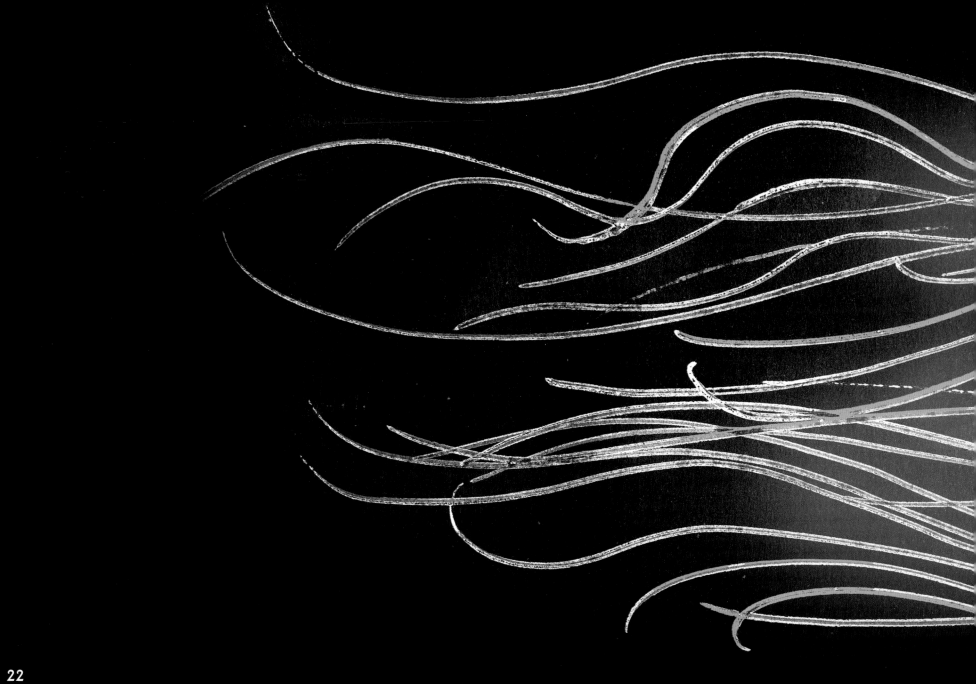

Crystal jellyfish shimmer.

Light bulbs glow.

Fireworks explode.

Stars twinkle.

Natural sources of light include the sun, the aurora borealis, lightning, fire, and bioluminescent plants and animals.

The sun is a star. It is the main source of light on Earth.

We see other stars at night. They are in the sky during the day, too, but we cannot see them because the sun is so bright.

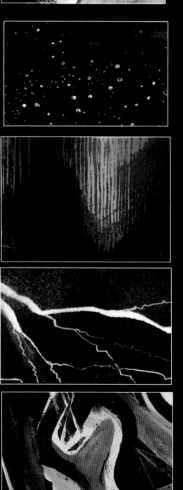

The aurora borealis is also called the northern lights. Particles from the sun mix with particles in the Earth's atmosphere and light up the sky.

Lightning strikes when negative charges from clouds meet positive charges from Earth—through buildings, trees, and even people. Lightning can also take place inside a cloud.

Fire needs fuel, oxygen, and heat. Paper, oils, wood, gases, fabrics, liquids, plastics, and rubber can be fuels.

Bioluminescence **is when plants, animals, and other living things produce light.**

Fireflies, *Mycena singeri*, **clusterwink snails, dinoflagellate plankton, firefly squids, and crystal jellyfish are bioluminescent.**

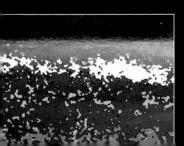

Artificial light is light made by humans. Light bulbs and fireworks are examples of artificial light.

BIBLIOGRAPHY

Johnson, Robin. *Catch a Wave: The Science of Light Waves.*
Crabtree Publishing Company, 2017.

Kukla, Lauren. *Light at Work.* Abdo Publishing, 2016.

The Exploratorium. *Exploring the Science of Light.* Weldon Owen, 2015.

Trumbauer, Lisa. *Rookie Read-About Science: All About Light.*
Scholastic, 2004.

White, Nancy. *The Magic School Bus Gets a Bright Idea: A Book About Light.*
Scholastic, 1999.

Whiting, Jim. *Mysteries of the Universe: Light. Creative Education,*
The Creative Company, 2013.

Wick, Walter. *A Ray of Light.* Scholastic Press, 2019.

Zimmer, Marc. *Bioluminescence: Nature and Science at Work.*
Twenty-First Century Books, 2015.

WEBSITES:

"Fire Facts for Kids." sciencekids.co.nz.
https://www.sciencekids.co.nz/sciencefacts/fire.html

"Light." dkfindout.com.
www.dkfindout.com/uk/science/light/

"What Causes the Sun to Give Off Heat?" space.com. March 1, 2012.
https://www.space.com/14735-sun-heat-source-explained.html

"Where Does the Sun's Energy Come From?"
spaceplace.nasa.gov. March 26, 2020.
https://spaceplace.nasa.gov/sun-heat/en/

INDEX

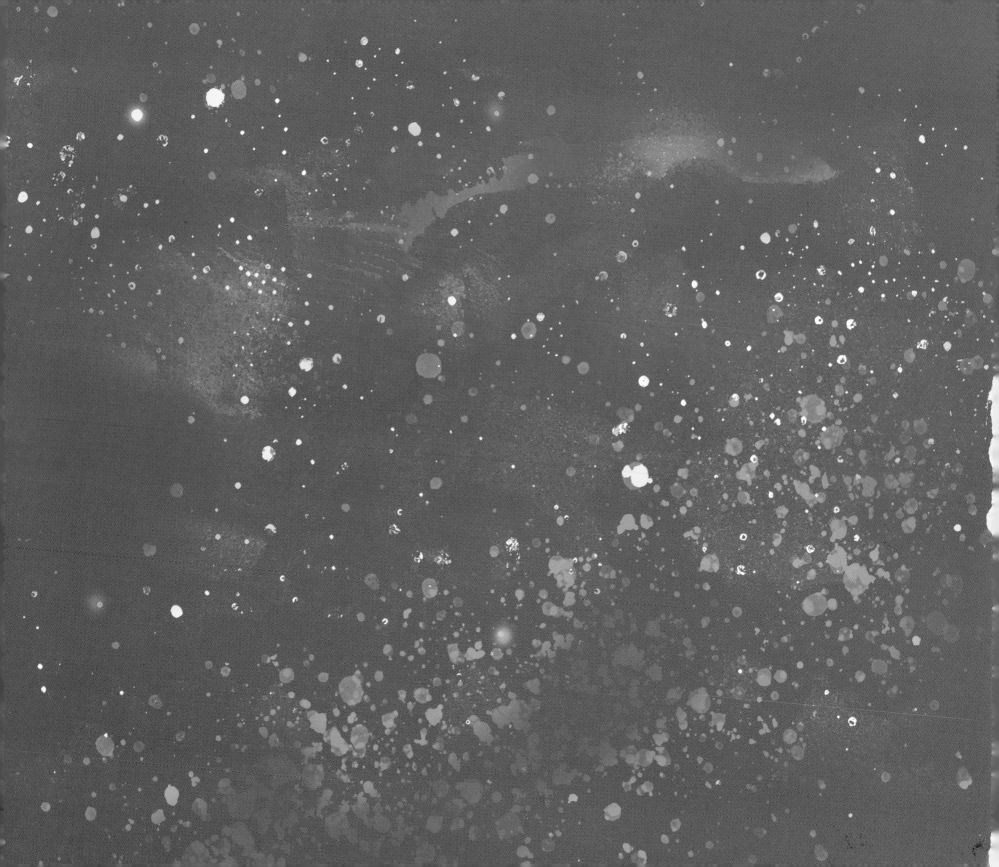